YOU

Trish N. Varner and Devon K. Varner

DEDICATION

We dedicate this book to one another, to our children, and to those we hope to inspire. Here is our love story to remember forever.

CONTENTS

ACKNOWLEDGMENTS

First, thank You God for bringing us into one another's lives, for selecting each of us for one another, and for knowing what we needed even when we didn't know. Thank You for being the center of us. We would also like to thank the strong marriages and examples we have in our lives. Thanks to Bruce and Beverly Galbreath for your love and support. Thanks to Bishop and Dr. Bessie Ludd for their guidance and encouragement and for teaching us how to become one.

1 SEARCHING

Are you somewhere searching for me?
Like I'm searching for you?
In my day dreams
Lying in bed at night
Driving down the road
Sitting at a park
Watching others
And their seemingly perfect love

Are you somewhere wondering like me?
How this thing
Supposedly so natural
Has bypassed yearly
Arrogantly and boldly
Without an excuse or apology
And happily lands
On those not even calling

Are you second guessing like me?
Every time a mirror says hi
And wondering if my appearance
Suits its standard
Or if my way or sway
Is enough to grab and keep
An interest in the mind
And perhaps spark a conversation

I wonder just how you will be
Not just your looks
Or the way you make a living

What you drive
The house in which you dwell
Your past
Or education
All these are important

But I wonder these things
What's on your mind?
What's in your heart?
What are your dreams?
Where in the world do you want to go?
How do you want to live as us?
But right now I'm searching

2 HAVE YOU SEEN HER?

I hear her soothing voice echo through my ears.
Like waves gently washing across the shore.
Her voice so calm and peaceful.
I so longingly adore.
Have you seen her?

I smell her pleasant air waft through my nose.
Like fresh summer roses still in the garden.
Her air so enticing and arousing.
I become enraptured and taken.
Have you seen her?

I feel her warm breath whisk across my neck.
Like a spring breeze across the country side.
Her breath so relaxing and tranquil.
I turn to see who resides.
Have you seen her?

I see her gorgeous frame blind my eyes.
Like the Earth, Moon, and Stars on an autumn night.
Her frame so breathtaking and magnificent.
I prepare my heart, mind, and soul for a fight.
Have you seen her?

I taste her supple lips against my own.
Like fresh spring strawberries from the Garden of Eden.
Her lips so delicious and tempting.
I stay for I have tasted the forbidden.
Have you seen her?

I hear her with my ears.
I smell her with my nose.
I feel her with my body.
I see her with my eyes.
I taste her with my lips.
I awake myself and ask,
Have you seen her?

3 NOT YOU

Give me the award now
For finding vessels
With the appearance of real
But having no real fit
Simply put, it's not you

My eyes lie to me
Having the nerve to smize
At encountering counterfeit
Representation of what could be
But it's not you

Here I am wondering
If perhaps
I might just settle
For lackluster love
Because it's not you

Wondering if my faith
Can sustain
Feelings of loneliness
Lacking your presence
Where are you?

Got me doing inventory
I'm fine…I think…check
I'm smart…I know…check
Spiritual walk strong…check
Still no you

This makes no sense
Years keep passing
Feeling older and refined
But still lacking that
Which is you

None has been
What I imagine you to be
None has shown
To be my complement
Seeing they're not you

How will I know when it is you?
Not sure really
All I know is you are not yet
So impatiently waiting
Cause none has been you

4 HE SAID

He said you'd be
About yay high
Broad shoulders
A little younger
Did He miss the memo?

I said I'd like
An older and distinguished
Chocolate skyscraper
Perhaps a little militant
Look at silly me

He pulled the omniscience card
How can I argue that one?
So I shut my mouth
And there you appeared
Exactly like He said

Do you know
You're the one
Foretold to walk this world
Hand in hand with me
Did you get the memo?

Did He tell you also?
What you're in for?
Should I share this news?
Hush me. We just met.
Look at silly me

What did you say?
You want to join my church?

That's a little quick
I'm giving you the side eye
But that is what He said

We will see
If you're the truth
We'll see where this goes
But I can't help wonder
You're the one He said

5 COULD IT BE

Something refreshing came this way
It was altogether sweet
From the scent of perfume
To the pretty smile
Could this be?

After walking a journey so long
With its incredible ups and downs
Looking for that perfect match
Could it be?

The conversation was right
She's got a mind that's also fine
It's not only her face
And physique attracting me
Got me wondering could this be?

Nothing extravagant happened
Yet it was altogether extraordinary
We talked and ate
Admired each other across the table
Could this be?

I feel I can tell her anything
I hope I didn't say too much
I will be doing everything
In my power
To discover could this be

If you are that one
I'm ready to love
I'm ready to hold on

I'm ready to give you all
If this could be

I think I'm going to
Dream well tonight
Meet her again there
Until I can see her again
Because I'm wondering could this be

6 FROM DAY ONE

From day one
You've been a little different
Not sure how to take that
Opening car doors
And every other door with a handle
Pulling out chairs
And listening intently
How long will that last?

I've always known God is real
I mean He's shown this many times
But you appearing like described
Got my mind blown
And wondering if this is
Some kind of trick
Or if you're someone superficial
Perhaps a fading façade

I'm the one usually
Laying down the limits
Of what I'm willing to deal with
Before moving on
But this time it's you
You're like no one I met before
Got me wondering what's going on

You said you're not into just hanging out
Not wanting something temporary
So you gave me a decision to make
Giving no other way
But exclusivity
Meaning we're on this ride

And I must make a choice
To be your lady and you my man

Not sure what's this I'm in
But something about the fact
You laid that down
Before any grey lines
Could be blurred
Earned you my respect
That I've never really given
I recognize the difference…so I say yes

From day one
You've been a little different
Couldn't quite pinpoint how
Then it hit me
You're a man
To the fullest extent
But not just any man either
A man chosen by God

7 STATUS CHANGE

This has just gotten real
Today Facebook asked me
To confirm our relationship
I mean I know we're in one
But now we're announcing it
All openly to the world

I will be revealed to all you know
You will be revealed to everyone else
You haven't met yet
Questions will be asked
Inquiring minds digging for info
This has just gotten real

Glad you don't want me hidden
Lets me know you're serious
About this thing called us
But I know you have a past
I do too but more settled perhaps
Can this…us openly stay?

See this status change
Brings a wealth of new things
A greater us to explore
But also throws us into a warzone
Where everyone can't see God working
And some just want to stop it

Can we weather this?
This is where we'll really be tested
To see if this relationship is real
And we are whom we say

If our testimony is true
And if we're validated by Him

This is where we'll either
Run to each other
Or turn from one another
Where outside forces
May find a way to infiltrate
This newness and beauty of us

Secretly I'm a little bit scared
Of what shall unfold
When I click and confirm
This Facebook status change
Because this is where faith gets real
Trusting God we'll be able to stand

I know what you'd say
It's just Facebook
How I wish it were as simple
As you present it
You're a little more optimistic
Than I about the intentions of people

Despite my hesitations
The thought of us is worth pursuing
Will you be the man
For whom I endured this 10 year wait
Only time will tell
Confirming this status change

8 GOODBYE

Sometimes change comes
With a rolling of a storm
Howling winds and rain
Threatening to knock down
Incorrectly built structures
But we're built on a Solid Rock
We make each other better
And I dare believe what He said

It's a peculiar thing to note
When those you least expected
Rise up and challenge a work of beauty
That's how I see the unfolding of us
No less than a magnificent beauty
That dare not be ignored or passed over
But must be embraced as once in a lifetime
Like planets that align or newly discovered stars

A beautiful thing must be respected
Anything contrary is a travesty of nature
For which endangered lists are formed
To prevent interrupting unique treasures
Not everyone can understand the value
Of distinct finds waiting for their unveiling
Leaving one true course for the misinformed
And that course ends in goodbye

Goodbye to those who use words
Like graffiti to defame our togetherness
Goodbye to the peace breakers

Who despise the very look of happiness
Goodbye to anything standing in the way
Of our happily ever after
Hello life anew and abundant
Declaring a beginning for every end

9 ONE OF THESE DAYS

One of these days I want to hold your hand as we talk and stroll
down the streets of cities we've never seen before
I want to stop and kiss you for no reason at all
under the favor of shiny stars
I want to whisper love in your ear
and then watch you blush
…and smile
as you draw me near
…to you
and hold me for awhile
I want to smile at your accomplishments
and be glad for you
I want to sit all day
and share things with you
I want to learn the things you like
and care for you
I want to be the one who's there for you
I like you on my mind
I like the feeling of your touch
I like the way you kiss
I like the uncontrolled rush
Hmmm...
One of these days
we'll make love with no limitations
You can choose the spot
and then when you're tired of that one
you can choose another
We won't ever have to stop
Let's climb with each other

until it becomes too much
until we are totally consumed
by the other's touch
until we no longer can detect
the start nor the end
Just one wave after the next
…and then after the next
…and after the next
You and I enjoying the ride
And then I….
will stay on board if you will
I won't stop if you don't
I'll go on if you go
Hmmm…
One of these days…
I just don't know
…if I can wait

10 THE WAIT

Yesterday I showed you
Me without eyebrows
Not sure what more you need
To know I'm serious about us

I'm comfortable with you
Even more than that actually
You make me feel safe
And surprisingly protected

I haven't laughed so much
We talk like we've known
Each other forever
Challenge each other for better

I've just got one question
What are we waiting for?
Knowing everything is right
Dare we take this next step?

You got me looking at everything
Wondering if this is the moment
Then each day comes to an end
And I realize the wait continues

Valentine's Day has arrived
This has to be the day!
Dinner and then the park
Waiting all day for the finale

You pull out a small box
I smile with excitement

Inside a beautiful heart
Wrapped around a necklace

I admire its beauty
Trying to hide disappointment
We are worth waiting for
So I continue to wait

11 PROPOSAL

My angel, look into that mirror and I will tell you what I see.

I see the love of my life
My one true love
The anchor of my soul
May we together continue to grow old

I see my better half
My shining star in the night
The soother of my wounded heart
May we never grow apart

I see the reason why I live
My excuse for making it through the day
The apple of my eye
May our love never go awry

I see the completion of my being
My queen in the chess game of life
The quencher of all my desires
May we continue to light each other's fires

Down deep in my soul
My love burns a fire untold
A fire that awaits for your eye only to see
My love, my heart, my soul, my every desire

I love you

12 EVERYDAY

Everyday I'm happy
Even when it doesn't appear that way
When I'm a little bratish (one who acts a little like a brat)
Or when I'm a little bit of this
Or a little bit of something else
In spite of all that....
Inside I still smile
....because I have you

Everyday I'm glad
To see your name
Appear on my screen
When you're calling me
Or every once in a while
When you sign on to send me a chat
I smile more when I see you
Walking toward me
It makes me blush
Inside and out....I smile
Because I have you

Everyday I long
To bring some joy to your life
To make you know everything is alright
To somehow someway make everything
Just a little brighter
Because I want to fully be
The blessing God promised to you
Demonstrate the love He's given me for you
All the while

The Love Project

I smile
Because I'm so glad to have you

Everyday I look for ways
To show you how much I care
To show you I'm always going to be here
To show you I'm thankful for this chance
This encounter in destiny
That has brought you to me
And I smile....
Big and long
Because I have you

You're the man
I asked for
And longed for
Prayed for
And cried for
Imagined at night
And thought of
In my daydreams
God, I'm so thankful
So I smile....
Inside and out
Because I'm so very glad
About all of the everydays
I have with you

13 THE WEDDING

It came so quick while also taking so long
This is the day I take on your name
Oh what a very beautiful thing
Nothing could ruin the moment
Even if it poured down rain and stormed
I'd still walk down that aisle
And stand by your side all smiles
And happily say I do
Happily say I will walk with you
Through this life and even longer
If given that chance
I'd have a hundred weddings with you
Standing in the mirror
Triple checking wedding day perfection
Reminiscing our journey
My eyes can't help but fill with tears
My heart can't help but feel
The excitement for our tomorrows
What our destiny shall reveal
How we shall grow and become one
Our loved ones all around
Their happiness for us is exuberant
An atmosphere so perfect
That even heaven rejoices and dances
I wait for the grand entrance
You make yours to the delight of everyone
I holding my daddy's hand
Breathe in once more and begin the walk
Purple and silver arrayed
Royalty and redemption tell our story
How God makes glorious
Renewed chances for the redeemed

Everything pure beauty
Gliding down the aisle watching you
You are consumed
By this destined moment in time
I see your face, you mine
Everyone else temporarily disappear
Your eyes draw me
Until there I stand together with you
We quiet nervousness
Together we are each other's strength
Your look approves
My look welcomes all that "us" offers
The preacher begins
Solidifying this union called before time
I do take you
You do take me to be your bride
We passionately kiss
Everything was worth this moment
A lifetime with you
Hand in hand we happily begin it

14 BECOMING ONE

Here we are in year one, my love
The wedding day
And all its magnificence
Is left in memory and pictures
We've crossed that threshold
To our humble abode
Where real tests begin
Of commitment, endurance
Where we find out
After the honeymoon is over
The things
That get under our skin
And the work
That we've really been called
To do for each other
For spiritual and natural growth
Marriage bootcamp
Where the goal is to become one
Not as in two halves
But as in power increasing power
Good things
Aren't created without struggle
Discomfort at times
Pushes the process forward
I'm convinced
We are coming out as pure Gold
Our story
Having already been settled
We keep focus
And that focus is on One
He is

The only One allowed in
He straightens
All wrongs and reminds us of love
He gives strength
To go above and beyond weaknesses
He is our center
The nucleus for the best of us
His loving way
Brings the most extraordinary success for us
I accept the journey
There is no one better I'd rather be with
Let's be a light
Loving each other and becoming one

15 YOU

Do you know
You're the woman
I would die for?
Do you know?
I searched for many years
Looking for someone special
Someone to share my life with
The woman for me
From my side
Taken from me
Someone who would ride
With the best of me
Choose to stay around
During the worst of me
Destined to lift me up
Encourage the man
God made me to be
Fulfilling God's plan
Hand in hand
In love as one

Do you know
You're the man
I was formed for?
Do you know?
I searched for many years
For a place
To pour all my love in
A friend
Soulmate
Lover
Explore the world with

Until I saw your face
And knew
It was you
God sent me to
You hold us up
I stand by your side
A love that's right
I call you Boaz
You call me bride

Do you know
It was God
That blessed this union?
Do you know?
He breathed his breath
In you, a man
Formed in His image
Said it was not good
To walk alone
Took a rib from his side
And made woman
Blessed them with dominion
To prosper
And multiply
Rule the world
Show His face
Demonstrate His grace
To walk in faith
He called you; He called me
Together as one

ABOUT THE AUTHORS

Trish and Devon Varner were married in 2010, one year after divinely meeting. Devon grew up in Georgia. Trish grew up in the Midwest and moved to Georgia in 2008. Natural poets, the couple wrote poems about one another prior to meeting and while dating. They are the founders and owners of VaFuGa Group, LLC a firm that specializes in business consulting services. They also own and operate VaFuGa Group Publishing. Devon has a Master's in Information Systems and Trish has a Master's in Business Administration and is studying for a PhD in I/O Psychology. They have two children together and four brought into the marriage.

www.ingramcontent.com/pod-product-compliance
Lightning Source LLC
Chambersburg PA
CBHW071449040426
42445CB00012BA/1487